Celebrations of Faith

60 Banner Designs

Carla Krazl

CPH
SAINT LOUIS

To the praise and honor of our God.

1   2   3   4   5   6   7   8   9   10   08   07   06   05   04   03   02   01   00   99

Table of Contents

Preface

So what exactly is a "Celebration of Faith"? Perhaps your first thought would be of thankfulness and praise to God for the faith He gives or simple joy from knowing of the eternal life we will receive. This is true, yet there is so much more!

Any occasion that we as Christians celebrate is a celebration of our faith! Any celebration happens because someone has received a blessing. Blessings come from God, our Savior. And our faith surely rests in Him. A wedding, baptism, or anniversary; stewardship and family life; communion and prayer—these are all blessings from the Lord and all celebrations of faith. When looked at in this light, celebrations of faith occur every day in our lives and in the church. Now you have the opportunity to enrich the service of celebration with a beautiful, creative, visual statement—a banner.

Your creation will be a focal point for the congregation and a source of joy and love for the person(s) it will be specially made for.

There is going to be a celebration!

May God bless your work as you labor out of love for Him and your brothers and sisters in Christ.

Let
Your
Light
Shine

Construction Guidelines

Getting Started

Selecting a banner to make is sometimes the most difficult part of the project. The table of contents categorizes the banners for quick reference. If your celebration is somewhat nonspecific (praise, family life, etc.), flip through the book and look for possibilities under other sections. Some banners would be appropriate for multiple occasions. One consideration as you choose which design to construct should be whether the banner (or group of banners) will appropriately fit in the designated hanging location. If the banner is being made as a gift for someone, ask him or her if they have a preference.

Can't decide? Often the best choice is the banner design that comes to life in your imagination—the one that can already be pictured in color. Keep in mind this is *your* creation. Feel free to modify a design if it does not look quite "right."

Enlarging the Pattern

After choosing a banner design, the first step is to enlarge the line drawing to an actual-size pattern. It is best (and easiest in the long run) to draw **two** full-size patterns. One will be used as a pattern for cutting fabric to the appropriate shapes; the other will be used as a guide for placing the pieces on the banner background.

Enlarging can be done in either of two ways:

1. Using a Projector

Chances are that an opaque projector or overhead projector will be available in the church or school office. An opaque projector displays the design onto a wall using a paper copy. An overhead projector does the same with a copy of the design on a transparency (also available from the church office or a quick-copy store).

Project the banner design onto a blank wall in a semidark room. Move the projector toward or away from the wall to change the size of the image. Use a tape measure to be exact and ensure the projection is "square." (Fig.1) Tape a piece of butcher paper (or disposable tablecloth, wrapping paper, or even sheets of newsprint) to the wall and trace the design. Turn off the projector and make sure nothing has been missed.

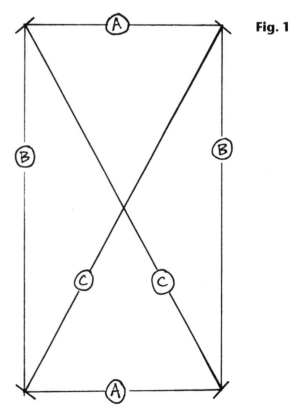

Fig. 1

Opposite sides should be equal.
Diagonals should be equal.

This pattern will remain uncut and serve as the "placement pattern."

Take down pattern #1 and tape up another piece of paper. This time, carefully trace all elements except the plain (non-decorative) letters. Instead, draw a box around them. Check for missing elements and remove the pattern. This "cut-up pattern" will be used to cut the design pieces from fabric. Try to avoid folding the patterns. Roll them up and hold them with a rubberband.

Back to those omitted letters ... trace them onto separate paper. They will be used individually, so paper scraps can be used. Be sure all the letters get traced. (Fig. 2)

2. Using a Grid

No projector? No problem. True, it is a bit more time consuming, but the advantage is that the design can be easily modified to fit your ideas.

Photocopy both the design from the book and the grid pattern on page 88. Tape the design over the grid so they line up and you can see the grid through the design. Determine how big the finished banner is to be. For example, one grid square could be equal to six inches of life-size banner. Keeping equal proportions, lightly draw a larger grid onto butcher (or similar) paper using a yardstick. The kitchen floor is usually an ideal place to do this because the linoleum or tile provides a "square" pattern. Make sure your pattern is square by measuring diagonals. (See Fig. 1) Use a pencil to enlarge the design onto the butcher paper using the grids as guides. Don't be shy about using an eraser!

A duplicate pattern should be made as outlined in "Using a Projector." An easy way to accomplish this is by laying tissue paper over the enlarged design and tracing carefully.

Fig. 2

placement pattern

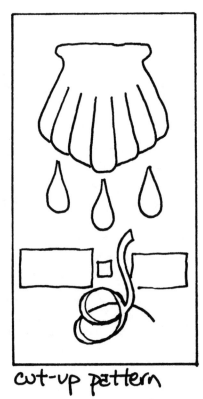

cut-up pattern

letter patterns

Choosing Fabric

The fabric store can be an overwhelming place. The best thing to do is to take some time and browse. Make sure to have your design in hand! When choosing a background fabric, notice that types of fabrics hang differently. Some heavyweight fabrics, such as cotton duck and denim, heavy felt, upholstery fabric, and drapery, do not need to be lined. Mediumweight fabrics are also good for backgrounds: poplin, twill, polyester/ rayon blends, and satin.

All of these fabrics can be used for the design elements. The background and elements can be the same type of material or they can be different types. Occasionally a banner will lend itself to the use of more unique choices: calico, terry cloth, plush felt, metallic fabrics, and taffeta.

Measure before you buy! The full-size pattern is drawn before the trip to the fabric store for a reason. Using a yardstick, make notes in the margin of the book's design of approximately how much fabric each element will need. Running short of fabric when the banner is almost done is a hassle! Always buy extra to accommodate test gluing/coloring.

Also consider lining requirements when purchasing fabrics. Some background fabrics can be lined using fusible interfacing (available by the yard). Others can be double-layered. If the background fabric is dark, some light-colored design pieces may need to be double-layered to preserve their color. Account for this when purchasing material. Also allow for fabric shrinkage; all washable fabrics should be preshrunk before anything is marked or cut.

Some fabrics are not suitable for banners. Knit, stretchable fabric, corduroy, and velvet are all hard to glue and can be ruined by an iron.

Choosing Colors

The wedding banner is definitely easiest to select colors for. Just ask the bride! Color choices for the rest of the banners might be more challenging.

If fabrics came only in the colors of a crayon eight-pack, explaining color choices for banners would be easy. But they do not. Fabrics are available in a huge range of colors, shades, textures, and prints. Spelling out all the right choices for banner-making would take another whole book. Instead consider the following guidelines when making color selections:

- Color is certainly a personal choice.

- Color sets the mood of the banner: vivid colors for joyful and cheerful feelings, dark colors for somber moods, pastels for peace and contentment.

- Providing contrast is a must, especially for legible words. A light background of white or pastel combined with black, dark purple, green, or blue design elements is a good choice. A dark background with light design elements also gives contrast, but remember that light fabrics often need to be lined to preserve their color when glued to a dark fabric.

- When shopping, ask a store employee for swatches cut from the bolts you are considering for letters and design elements. Unroll a yard or two of the background fabric and lay the swatches on top. Stand back from your choices and see which look the best from a distance.

- For subtle variations, try using fabrics of the same color but different shades, or calico prints and solid colors in the same color family.

- Felt is very easy to work with, especially for detailed, fancy lettering. Fraying is never a worry!

- Kids love textures.

- Metallics are great additions. Shiny fabrics provide elegance and are surprisingly easy to work with when using iron-on fusible web.

Born of
Water
& Spirit

Stephen John
August 8, 2003

GROW IN CHRIST

02

SAINT THOMAS HIGH

Lessons in Lettering

Fig. 3

Many of the banners in this book have space for personalization. Including the name of the person(s) who is celebrating the faith makes the banner personal and turns it into a cherished gift as well. With some simple "planning ahead" steps, adding a name to a banner is easy.

Some alphabet outlines can be found on pages 84-87. It is generally best to choose a letter style that matches letters used in other words of the banner or that provides a noticably different style to those other letters. (Fig. 3)

Once a letter style is selected, make photocopy enlargements of the chosen alphabet to the size needed. Determine the necessary size by measuring the sample name in the enlarged pattern. Follow the banner design's lead of using all capital letters or upper- and lowercase letters.

Using the photocopies, trace the words onto plain paper. Lay this tracing on the full size banner pattern to make sure the letters fit properly. Reduce the size of the letter patterns if necessary. Keep these patterns for use with future banners.

When gluing these letters onto your banner, space them by eye. Do not use a ruler to measure space between letters. Imagine filling the spaces between letters with sand. Each space should get the same amount of sand. (Fig. 4) It is, however, a good idea to use a ruler as a baseline guide. Be aware that round letter go lowers and higher than square letters. (Fig. 5)

Fig. 4

Andrew

Julie

Fig. 5

Whenever working with words, **always step back and check your spelling and spacing before gluing!**

Getting to Work

The patterns and the fabrics are ready. Finding a place to work is the next task. A large, flat spot such as a Ping-Pong table, dining room table, or even the kitchen floor will work. The ironing board set to the same height and next to the kitchen table can do in a pinch.

The Background

Before marking the fabric, make sure the paper pattern is square. A tile or linoleum floor works well because of the geometric shapes in the flooring itself. Line up the pattern with the squares in the floor. Everything should be even. (Fig. 6)

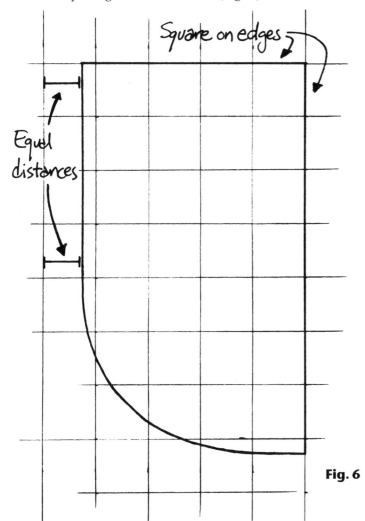

Fig. 6

If the pattern is not square, carefully trim the uneven edges. This is the best way to check banners with rounded bottoms. Another method of checking "square" is to use a tape measure. Lengths of opposite sides and diagonals should be equal. (See Fig. 1)

Lay the fabric face down on the floor or table. Unroll the "placement pattern" on top, also face down. Secure the pattern to the fabric with a few pins. Using a pencil, mark the cut lines around the pattern, adding 3" to the top, 1 1/2" to the bottom, and 1/2" to both sides. Trim the fabric along the lines.

Drape the background fabric over a rod to see how it hangs. Is it flat? Or is it waving and/or curling? If the fabric is sturdy and already hangs nicely, the banner will not need a lining. If the background fabric is medium- or lightweight, a lining will cause it to hang much nicer.

1. Unlined

Machine stitch a 1/2" hem down both sides, then a 1 1/2" hem on the bottom. For the hanging casement, lay the fabric face down. Mark a line 6" from the top. (Be sure the mark does not bleed through the fabric.) Fold down the fabric to the line and stitch. Leave the sides of this top hem open to allow the hanging rod to slide through. Strips of iron-on adhesive can be used to hem the sides and bottom. The top hem should be sewn to bear the banner's weight when displayed.

2. Fusible Interfacing Lining

Hem the banner according to the method for unlined banners. With the hems in place, iron fusible interfacing over the back of the entire banner. This interfacing is available by the yard in fabric stores, typically in 22" widths. Carefully follow the directions provided with the interfacing and practice on scraps first. When meeting two pieces of interfacing, overlap them *ever so slightly*.

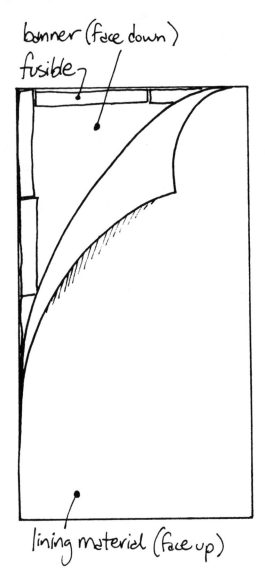

banner (face down)

fusible

lining material (face up)

3. Lightweight Fabric Fusing

Do not sew any hems. Cut a piece of fabric the same size as the banner background. This second piece could be cut from the same fabric or from a similarly colored fabric. Lay the banner fabric face down with the lining fabric face up directly on top. Lift the edges and slide strips of iron-on fusible web (such as Stitch Witchery) between the fabrics. Iron the three layers together according to the directions. (Fig.7) Neatly trim any edges that did not meet together exactly. There is no need to hem the edges, but the hanging casement does need to be made. Lay the banner face down. Mark a line 6" from the top. Fold down the fabric to the line and stitch.

4. Machine Stitch Lining

Do not sew any hems. Cut a piece of fabric the same size as the banner. The fabric can be the same as the background or another like-colored fabric. Pin the two pieces together, right sides facing each other. Machine stitch the sides and bottom 1/2" and 1 1/2" from the edges, respectively. Turn right side out and press the edges. To make the hanging casement, lay the banner face down and mark a line 6" from the top. Fold the fabric down to the line and stitch.

Fig. 7

The Design Pieces

Cutting out the Elements

Before cutting, write a corresponding number for each piece on the "cut-out" and the "placement" pattern. On the "cut-out" pattern, indicate the top of each piece with an arrow.

If the elements do not overlap, loosely cut around them. If they do overlap, cut the pattern on the line and indicate where you should add 1/4" to the piece that goes behind. Another option is to trace another pattern to make two pieces instead of three. (Fig. 8)

Fig. 8

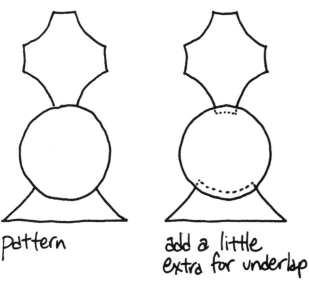

pattern   add a little extra for underlap   or make one continuous piece

Wash, dry, and iron any washable fabrics that will be used for design pieces. If the pieces will be attached with a fusible interfacing (such as Pellon Wonder-Under), iron it to the wrong side of the fabric according to the directions on the package.

There are two ways to go about cutting out the elements.

1. Cut out the paper pattern exactly. Using a visible pencil or pen, trace around the pattern onto the wrong side of the fabric or the paper backing of the fusible intrefacing. When tracing onto the back of fabric, be sure to turn the pattern face down also. To avoid tracing, pin the pattern to the fabric and carefully trim.

2. Loosely cut out the paper pattern. Pin the pattern to the fabric and cut pattern and fabric at the same time. Be aware that cutting paper dulls a scissors faster than cutting fabric. A scissors that cuts both will need to be sharpened more frequently than one that cuts only fabric.

If there is space available, keep the placement pattern out for the duration of the project. When each piece is cut out, lay it in its place on the pattern to keep them organized.

Attaching the Elements

Banners put together with iron-on adhesives generally look better and work cleaner than those assembled with glue. Fusibles are slightly more expensive than glue, and some fabrics with a nap (such as corduroy and velvet) cannot take an iron and must be glued. Always test on scrap fabric before committing to either method!

1. Glue

Thick craft glue, as opposed to school glue, is best for gluing banners.

Lay the background flat and arrange all the elements in place. Use the placement pattern as a reference. If precision is desired, use a ruler to measure distances from the edges to the piece on the pattern. Then duplicate these measurements on the banner. Begin by gluing any bottom layer elements. Hold down one side of the piece with a ruler, fold over one side, smooth on a bead of glue, and return the piece to its position. Do the same for the other side of the piece. Use care to use *enough* glue but not so much that the glue will bleed through to the surface.

2. Fuse

When using iron-on fusible web, preparing to attach fabric is a bit more crucial than when gluing. It is best to set the ironing board at the same height as a large table on which the banner is lying flat. First, lay any large background pieces in place. Use a ruler, if necessary, as described in the previous section on gluing. Pull the banner over the ironing board section by section and iron as you go. (Fig. 9) When background pieces are fixed, lay the banner on the table again and arrange the rest of the pieces. Repeat the process of ironing section by section working toward the top. Always refer to the package for instructions.

3. Stitch

Sewing the pieces onto the banner is a time-consuming job. But it is also the most elegant way to make a beautiful banner. It is a good idea to back each piece with fusible interfacing to prevent fraying edges.

The Finishing Touches

The details added at the end of banner-making are the finishing touches that pull everything together. Strength can be added to some design elements if they are outlined. The outlines can be glued on yarn, ribbon, or strips of felt. Paint is another option and can be brushed on or squeezed on. Outline elements the same color, but a darker shade, as the element to be outlined. Black is nearly always a good choice. Thin gold cord can also be a classy finish. Use your imagination—affix buttons, sequins, cotton, or beads where you think appropriate.

Perhaps the best way to see what finishing touches are needed is to hang the banner and step back as far as possible. Or lay the banner on the floor and look at it from across the room while standing on a chair. Try laying down some "finishing touches." See what looks good. But show some restraint. It can be easy to get carried away and end up with a banner that looks gaudy.

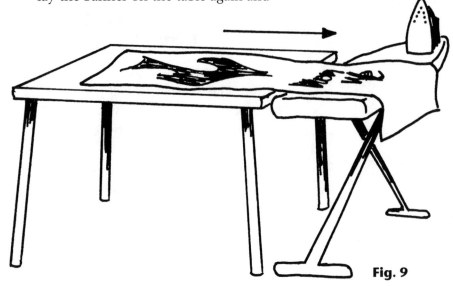

Fig. 9

Hanging Your Work

Almost every banner is hung by a dowel rod. A 3/4" wooden dowel is the standard. Simply slip the dowel through the banner's hanging casement. The banner can now be hung in several different ways.

Methods of Display

1. From the Wall

Securely mount two appropriately sized curtain rod hooks into the wall. Set the banner's dowel rod in the hooks. The hooks are permanent and can hold a variety of future banners. (Fig. 10)

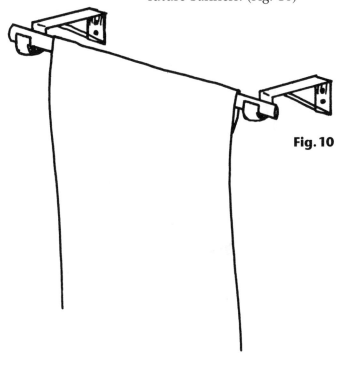

Fig. 10

2. From the Ceiling

Find a brave soul to climb to the ceiling to attach two lengths of 15 lb. test fishing line. Tie an "S" hook at the end of each line that can accommodate the banner's dowel rod. These lines can also be permanent and will very rarely be noticed, even without a banner hanging from them.

3. From a Pole

This is the most common and most versatile method of hanging. A cord or rope is attached to the dowel and then looped through a pole's hook. There are many types of rope available at fabric stores. Browse through the bolts and select one that complements the banner. Often white or gold is the best choice. Purchase enough to accommodate the width of the banner, plus hanging distance, plus any length wanted down the sides. (Fig. 11)

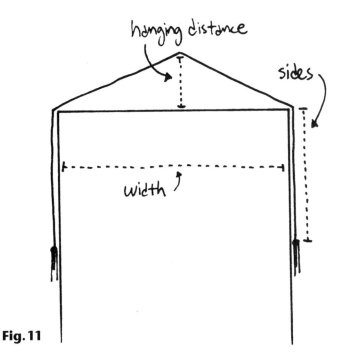

Fig. 11

Attach an eye screw at each end of the dowel. This should be done before sliding it through the banner's casement. Thread the cord through each eye screw and knot the cord at the point it should hang. (Fig. 12)

To prevent the banner from shifting (especially for processional banners), tie one overhand knot in the middle of the cord. Use the resulting loop to hang on the pole's hook.

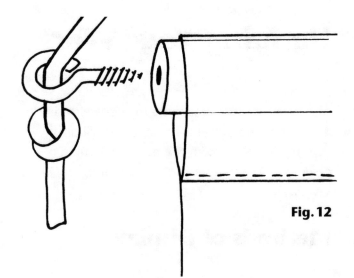

Fig. 12

Making a Pole Stand

If there is no banner pole stand available, a little more work needs to be done. Some basic carpentry skills and the following diagram will provide a durable, functional stand. (Fig. 13) The base should measure 18" x 18". The center square that holds the pole should be 18" tall.

The pole itself can be wood, metal, or PVC. A hook should be fastened to the top to provide a place to hang the banner from.

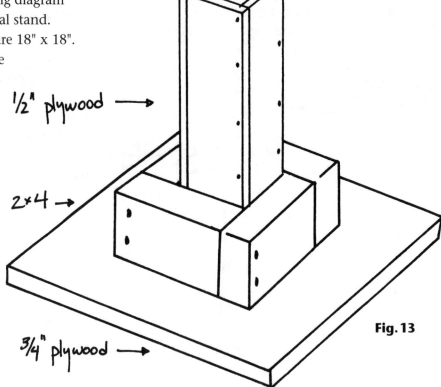

½" plywood →

2×4 →

¾" plywood →

Fig. 13

Banner Designs

Anniversary

A faithful man will be richly blessed.
Proverbs 28:20

Tips & Extras ~~~~~~

- The anniversary banners can be used for any anniversary—church founding, years in the ministry, wedding, even birthday.

- Try using gold for the circle burst behind the year.

- Make sure the fabric colors for the background and cross provide suitable contrast for the words at the bottom. If they do not, leave a section of the cross out, as illustrated on the white-background banner above.

- Explore different cords and ribbons for lining the cross and circles.

- Additional numbers can be found on page 82.

Celebrating God's Blessings FOR 50 YEARS

Michael † Carolyn

Tips & Extras ~~~~~

- As shown, this banner is for a couple's anniversary. The banner would be suitable for a church anniversary by omitting the cross and rings and adding the church's name if desired.

- Add glitter to the numbers to give them some punch. Cut the numbers from cotton fabric. Lay out a large area of waxed paper. Water down some school glue. Spread glue thinly on fabric using a paintbrush. Sprinkle glitter over fabric. Allow to dry before moving from waxed paper. The impact of the glitter on the banner can be toned down by using fabric of the same color for the words.

- Additional numbers can be found on page 82.

Anniversary

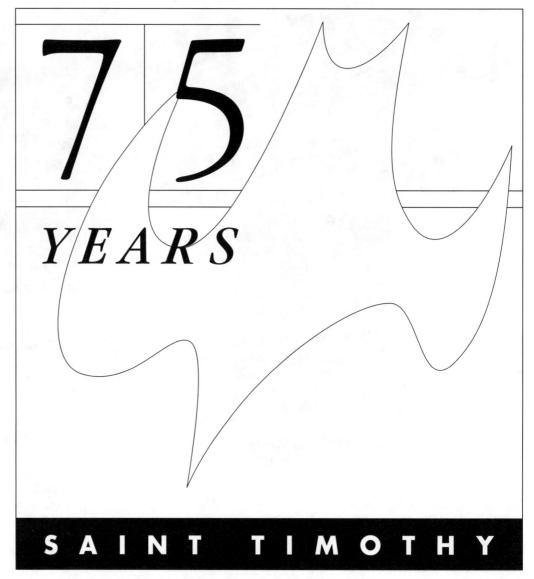

Tips & Extras

- The dove is a symbol for God the Holy Spirit, who has showered His children with countless blessings.

- This banner could be made for a church's anniversary and hung in the entryway, vestibule, or narthex for the entire celebration year.

- Consider using cut vinyl from a sign shop to make weatherproof banners for the light poles along the street or parking lot.

- An elegant banner could be made using only three colors. Experiment with markers before making a final choice.

- Additional numbers can be found on page 83.

John Stephen
July 25, 2004

Baptism

Therefore, if anyone is in Christ, he is a new creation; the old has gone, the new has come!

2 Corinthians 5:17

For you have been born again, not of perishable seed, but of imperishable, through the living and enduring word of God.

1 Peter 1:23

Tips & Extras 〜〜〜

- Use bright, vivid colors or patterns for the butterfly. No need to be conservative!
- Be sure to use contrasting colors so the cross stands out.
- Omit the name to make this a banner to be used by anyone.
- Read the "Tips & Extras" sections with the other baptism banners for ideas on personalized/community-use banners.

Baptism

"I tell you the truth, no one can enter the kingdom of God unless he is born of water and the Spirit. Flesh gives birth to flesh, but the Spirit gives birth to spirit."

John 3:5-6

Tips & Extras 〜〜〜

- To make a banner as a gift, personalize it with the name and date directly on the background of the banner. You may choose to use one background color or add a second color field (as shown above).

- Make a banner that can be kept at the church to be used for any baptism by simply omitting the person's name

- It is possible to make a "church" banner a personalized banner as well. The bottom section is not glued onto the background, but attached with Velcro instead. This bottom section can then become the congregation's gift to its newest member—simply follow the diagram below. Attach Velcro to the left side of the name section to form a simple hanging casement. Have a dowel rod and ribbon prepared and convert the banner after the service.

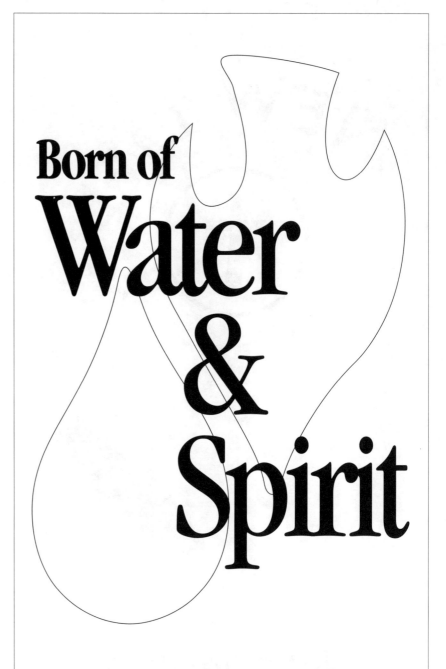

Born of
Water
&
Spirit

Stephen John
August 6, 2003

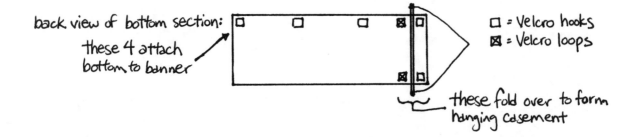

back view of bottom section:
these 4 attach bottom to banner

▢ = Velcro hooks
⊠ = Velcro loops

these fold over to form hanging casement

Born Of

Thomas James
Aug. 8, 2002

Baptism

"I tell you the truth, no one can enter the kingdom of God unless he is born of water and the Spirit. Flesh gives birth to flesh, but the Spirit gives birth to spirit."

John 3:5-6

Tips & Extras

- This banner is intended to be personalized. However, only the bottom piece is to be re-made for each new baptism—the top two pieces are re-used.

- There are three sections to the banner. The top two have a hanging casement and dowel rod at the top and bottom. It is not necessary to put a dowel rod at the bottom of the third section. Connect the panels with short lengths of cord screwed into the dowel rods. Tie knots in the cord before attaching to prevent fraying. Instead of cord, try a few links of decorative chain. A variety is available at any hardware store.

- The bottom section can be given to the newly baptized person. When the section is removed, attach a cord so the section can hang independently. It is also possible to have a water and dove shape ready to glue on the bottom section after the service. This gives a visual reminder of what celebration the banner represents.

Baptism

I am Jesus' little lamb, Ever glad at heart I am; For my Shepherd gently guides me, Knows my need and well provides me, Loves me ev'ry day the same, Even calls me by my name.

Lutheran Worship #517
Henrietta L. von Hayn

Tips & Extras

- Use cotton balls on white felt to make the sheep. Outline the fleece in black.
- One attractive color scheme option is pastel blue for the top and bottom, pastel yellow behind the sheep, and bright purple for the letters.
- Make a small version of the banner to be displayed in a child's room (18" x 27").

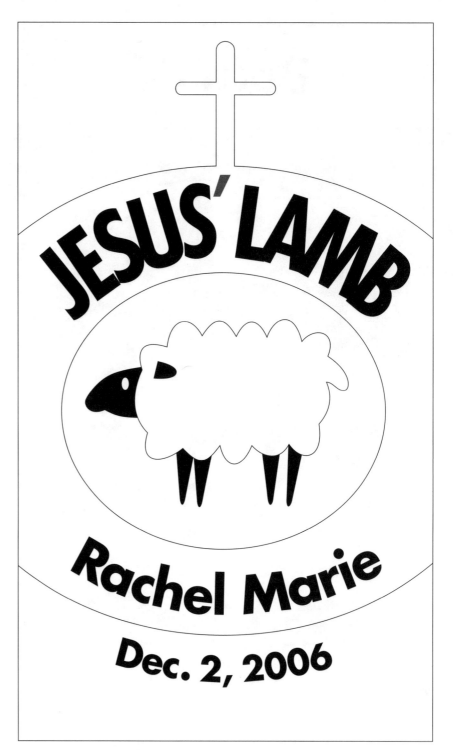

Baptism

"I tell you the truth, no one can enter the kingdom of God unless he is born of water and the Spirit. Flesh gives birth to flesh, but the Spirit gives birth to spirit."

John 3:5-6

Tips & Extras 〜〜〜〜

- An additional shell option is available below. Use your favorite.
- Some color scheme ideas: Light blue background, white shell and water drops, purple letters.
- White background, tan shell, light blue water, dark blue letters.
- Gold background, white shell and water, dark color letters.

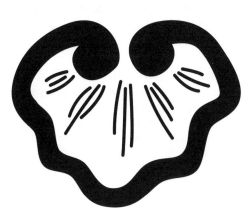

Baptism

"Go and make disciples of all nations, baptizing them in the name of the Father and of the Son and of the Holy Spirit, and teaching them to obey everything I have commanded you."

Matthew 28:19

Tips & Extras

- This banner can be personalized or left blank for general use in the church.
- Make a personalized banner, perhaps 2-3 feet tall, for display at home.
- Make the three bands three different dark colors. The letters are all white. The water drops could be silver lamé with white outlines and highlights.
- An additional color option: Above the water drops is all yellow. The letters are all a dark color. The water drops could be light blue. The dividing lines between the names are white, as well as the droplet highlights and outlines.

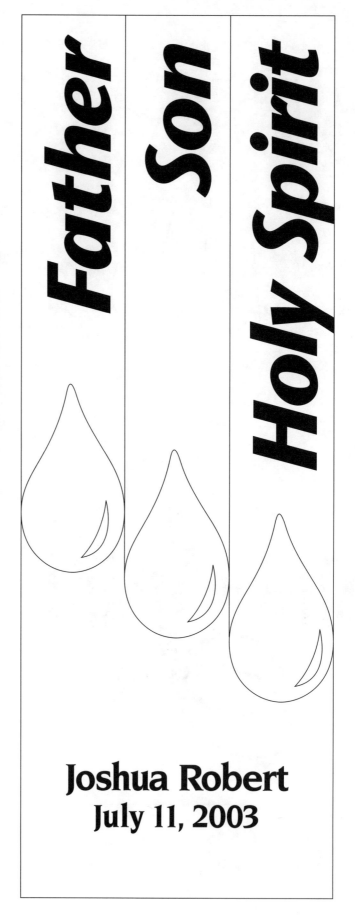

TRAIN A CHILD

IN THE WAY

PROVERBS 22:6

Train a child in the way he should go, and when he is old he will not turn from it.

Proverbs 22:6

Tips & Extras

• The background could be two similar fabrics: Dark blue and dark green, both dark purple with similar calicos, bright yellow and light orange. Sew two pieces together or use iron-on fusible to affix the top color to the background color.

• Easier background? All one color!

• Make this banner to hang in the front entrance of a Christian elementary school.

• Make a 4' banner for a child's classroom or as a gift for the teacher.

Christian School

"Red and yellow, black and white, all are precious in His sight: Jesus loves the little children of the world."

A song I remember from Sunday school

Tips & Extras ～～～

- The four circles represent four races; the colors should be different flesh tones.
- The cross could be gold and the background circle silver. The letters and accent dots can be the same fabric, perhaps blue in color.
- Use this banner as a chapel topic telling of Jesus' saving love for everyone.
- Hang this banner prominently in any culturally diverse environment.

EPHESIANS 3:14-19

Christian School

And I pray that you, being rooted and established in love, may have power, together with all the saints, to grasp how wide and long and high and deep is the love of Christ.

Ephesians 3:17-18

Tips & Extras

- Each class (day school, preschool, Sunday school, etc.) could have a flower with all the childrens' names on the petals.
- Another option: Carry out a school year theme by adding a flower each month during a chapel service that centers on an aspect of God's love.
- The flowers should be a variety of colors.
- The background could be white, the letters dark brown, and the dirt various shades of brown and tan. No need to follow the pattern with the dirt—just add until it looks right, making sure not to hide the letters in the process.

Commissioning

For we are God's workmanship, created in Christ Jesus to do good works, which God prepared in advance for us to do.

Ephesians 2:10

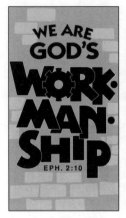 

Tips & Extras ~~~~

- The background and bricks should be colors that are similar in value. A tan background with off-white bricks or dark red background with patterned burgundy bricks would both look nice.

- The letters should contrast with the background. Outline them in white or black yarn to make them stand out even more.

- Try using silver lamé for the 'o' (to look like a metal gear).

Commissioning

Then He said to His disciples, "The harvest is plentiful but the workers are few. Ask the Lord of the harvest, therefore, to send out workers into His harvest field."

Matthew 9:37-38

Tips & Extras ～～～

- The wheat can be made with one color (golden yellow) or with two colors (light brown and golden yellow).

- The letters could be made from a bright color that complements the yellow wheat, such as dark purple.

- Give the wheat some visual texture by melting crayon shavings into yellow cotton fabric. Use a warm iron on these items (in bottom-to-top order): ironing board, waxed paper, fabric, shavings, waxed paper. Experiment with crayons in the brown and yellow families. Use the shavings sparingly; it is difficult to bond saturated, waxy fabric to the background using craft glue. Cut out the design shapes after melting the shavings.

Confirmation

"Be faithful, even to the point of death, and I will give you the crown of life."

Revelation 2:10

 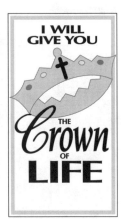

Tips & Extras ~~~~~

- On a light or dark background, use gold metallic fabric for the crown. Outline with a gold cord.

- The jewels could be made with colored glitter on colored fabric. Glue the glitter onto a cut-out shape before gluing to the banner itself. This keeps glitter from getting on everything.

- Use boldly colored felt for the letters.

- Add a finishing touch of gold cord or ribbon around the entire edge of the banner.

Confirmation

For it is by grace you have been saved, through faith—and this is not from yourselves, it is the gift of God—not by works, so that no one can boast.

Ephesians 2:8-9

Tips & Extras ~~~~

- Consider a dark, bold plaid for the "package." Use a coordinating wide ribbon to fashion a bow. Tack the bow in place with a few stitches or hot glue. Find a ribbon with wire in the edges— the bow will be easy to shape and will not sag when the banner is hung.
- Use a coordinating color for the top two color fields.
- Use a contrasting color for the letters. Outline with yarn, especially over the plaid fabric.

Confirmation

"Surely I am with you always, to the very end of the age.

Matthew 28:20b

Tips & Extras 〰️

- This banner is half of a pair. They could be hung anywhere together—on both sides of the chancel, in the back of the sanctuary (to see on the way out), the foyer (to see on the way in), etc.

- Use gold lamé, yellow, orange, or a combination of these for the sunburst. One way would be to use yellow fabric highlighted with orange and white crayon shavings (see "Tips & Extras" on page 33). Highlight only the rays, not the circle.

- Letters should be dark purple or dark green to complement the sun colors.

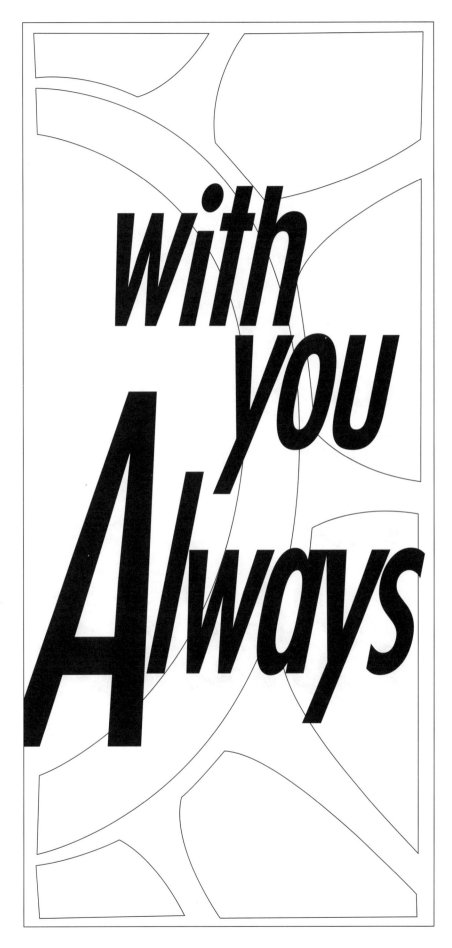

Confirmation

"Surely I am with you always, to the very end of the age.

Matthew 28:20b

Tips & Extras ∿∿∿

- This banner is the second half of a pair.
- Colors and fabrics should match the first banner; see "Tips & Extras" on the previous page.

Evangelism

"Neither do people light a lamp and put it under a bowl. Instead they put it on its stand, and it gives light to everyone in the house. In the same way, let your light shine before men, that they may see your good deeds and praise your Father in heaven."

Matthew 5:15-16

Tips & Extras ~~~~~

- Choose fabrics for the house from the same color family—different shades of tan, burgundy, or gray. Try letters of bright blue or dark green.

- The light spilling from the house should be bright yellow. Using a gold cord on the edge of the light will give it a strong accent. Be careful to use a gold that does not clash with the yellow fabric.

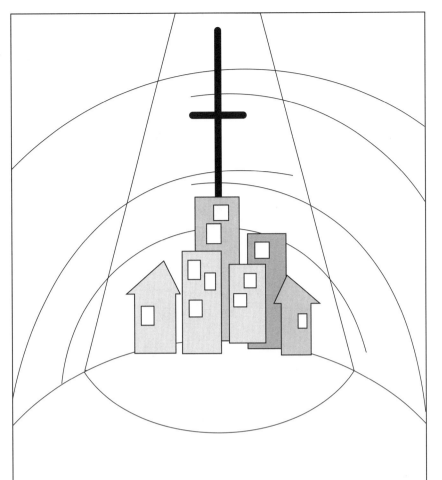

Evangelism

"You are the light of the world. A city on a hill cannot be hidden."

Matthew 5:14

Tips & Extras ~~~~

• Using regular fabrics: The light beam should be yellow and the hill green. The space where the light is shining onto the hill should be a lighter shade of green. The buildings can be browns and grays. The arcs in the sky could be gold cord or ribbon added as the final touch.

• Using yellow tulle (wedding veil) for the light: Cut out all the design pieces. Experiment with which elements (buildings, arcs, cross) look best above or beneath the netting. Glue down all pieces that look best beneath the netting. Machine stitch two, three, or four layers of netting onto the banner—just sew the edges. Finish by gluing on the remaining pieces (if any). There is no need to use a lighter green fabric for the area the light shines onto; the netting makes this area lighter.

Evangelism

Tips & Extras ~~~~

- Use glitter for the small circles surrounding the sun.

- Make the sun from yellow cotton fabric. Lightly highlight parts of the sun's rays with an orange watercolor marker. Use a wet paintbrush to blend the orange into the fabric. This will create some visual movement in the sun.

- Stand a good distance away from the banner to ensure the words stand out from the fabric. A white or black outline increases the contrast.

40

Family Life

So then, just as you received Christ Jesus as Lord, continue to live in Him, rooted and built up in Him, strengthened in the faith as you were taught, and overflowing with thankfulness.

Colossians 2:6-7

Tips & Extras ～～～

- To prevent a bulky double layer of fabric, join the "sky" and "ground" with one quick seam: Lay two fabrics right-sides together and stitch the edge that meets the two colors. Press the seam flat and then finish backing the banner, if desired.

- Experiment with colors at the fabric store. An option is to use the same color green and brown for the tree and trunk as for the ground and roots. Give the ground and roots a muted look by lightly spray painting with white, gray, or black. Be sure to cover the parts you do not want to paint!

- Use white for the letters. Outline in white to make them more bold.

Family Life

If I rise on the wings of the dawn,
if I settle on the far side of the sea,
even there Your hand will guide me,
Your right hand will hold me fast.

Psalm 139:9-10

Tips & Extras 〜〜〜〜

- Use a dark color fabric for the background and a slightly lighter shade of that color for the burst. This subtlety keeps the focus on the family, not the background. Use two different flesh colors for the hand and the family's heads.

- Outline the hand with a color slightly darker then the fabric. Use yarn, marker, or paint.

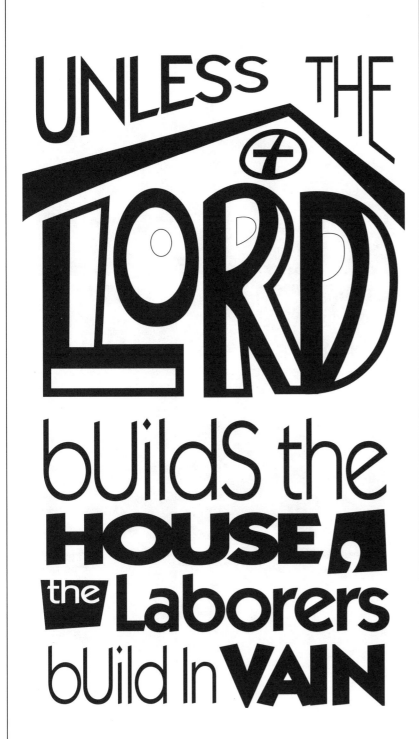

UNLESS THE LORD bUildS the HOUSE, the Laborers build In VAIN

Psalm 127:1

Unless the LORD builds the house, its builders labor in vain.

Psalm 127:1

Tips & Extras

- This banner could be used during a focus on family life, a wedding, a "Habitat for Humanity" program, building dedication, groundbreaking, etc.

- Select a few bright colors that harmonize. Make all the words (except "LORD") one color, the roof and two squares a second color, the "LORD" a third color, and the shapes that fill in "LORD" a fourth color. The small window under the roof could be the first color and filled in with yellow.

- These color suggestions are simply suggestions. Use markers and paper to try alternative color schemes before purchasing fabric.

Family Life

Tips & Extras 〜〜〜

- This banner could be used for a convocation weekend, retreat, or conference. It could also be used in a school setting or for "Family Faith Sunday."

- Keep the burst subtle by using yellow on a white background, for example, with burgundy letters.

- Or use a white background and do not use another color for the burst; outline it with gold cord. Simplify the burst as shown above. The cross and book cover could be brown, the family and letters a brighter, dark color.

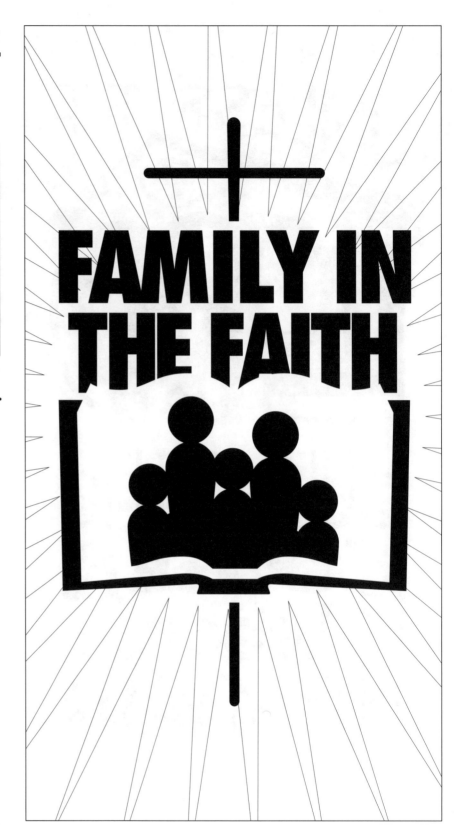

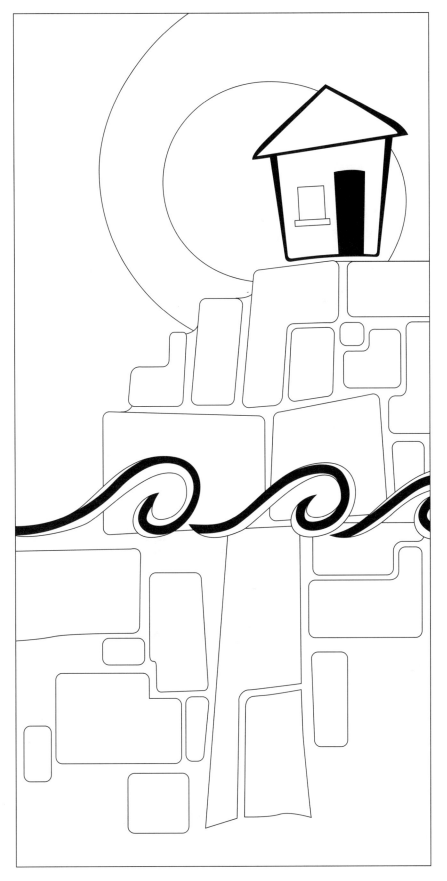

Family Life

"The rain came down, the streams rose, and the winds blew and beat against that house; yet it did not fall, because it had its foundation on the rock."

Matthew 7:25

Tips & Extras ~~~~

- See the cover of the book for one color scheme idea. This is done by selecting a color for behind the dry rocks, a second color for the rocks that make up the cross, and a third color for the rest of the dry rocks. Four colors are chosen for the water and wet rocks.

- Another way to differentiate the cross from the rocks: Select two fabrics for the dry area; one for the rocks and one for behind. Cut all the rocks from the same fabric, marking on the back which ones are for the cross. Outside, or in the garage, use white spray paint to lightly mist the cross rocks. Hold the can 18" above the fabric, barely pressing the tip so it spits, rather than sprays.

  Similarly, choose two fabrics for the wet area; one for the rocks and one for the water. Lightly paint the rocks that form the cross.

- Two ways to make the waves: 1) Cut white and light blue fabric just as the pattern indicates. 2) Cut each wave entirely out of white canvas fabric. Use watercolor paint to brush the blue highlight onto the wave. Use wispy, smooth strokes. Variety is good!

Funeral

Though outwardly we are wasting away, yet inwardly we are being renewed day by day. For our light and momentary troubles are achieving for us an eternal glory that far outweighs them all. So we fix our eyes not on what is seen, but on what is unseen. For what is seen is temporary, but what is unseen is eternal.

2 Corinthians 4:16-18

Tips & Extras

- Make the left half dark with light letters and the right half white with dark letters. This visually signifies the separation of death and eternal life.

- Make the left side background and the right side words the same color.

- The circle behind "Eternal" could be metallic gold lamé or bright yellow fabric.

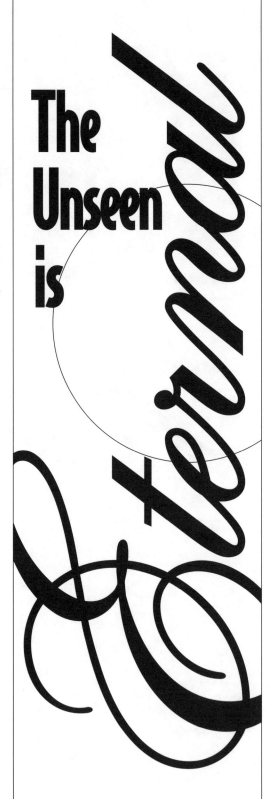

Funeral

Praise be to the God and Father of our Lord Jesus Christ! In His great mercy He has given us new birth into a living hope through the resurrection of Jesus Christ from the dead, and into an inheritance that can never perish, spoil or fade—kept in heaven for you.

1 Peter 1:3-4

Tips & Extras ~~~~~

• White background, yellow circle, dark letters (purple, navy, etc.), tan cross.

• For letters that will stand out more in the circle, outline them with white yarn or squeeze paint.

• Designs for altar and pulpit paraments are included here also. You will notice that a basic element of the design has simply been repeated in various size applications. For a cohesive look, use the same color scheme for all pieces of the group.

• A basic element of any banner design can be applied to altar and pulpit paraments in this same way.

Funeral

Jesus said to her, "I am the resurrection and the life. He who believes in Me will live, even though he dies; and whoever lives and believes in Me will never die."

John 11:25-26

Tips & Extras

- The background is an abstract of the empty tomb. Accentuate this by making the sky dark blue, the ground dark green and the tomb browns. The cross would be light tan; the letters and cloth would be white.

- Another option is to make the background all equal shades of medium to dark brown, gray and taupe. The cross, cloth, and letters would all be white. Experiment at the fabric store!

- Make the cloth actually drape by using thin fabric and sewing along the top edges only.

1 Cor. 15:56-57

The sting of death is sin, and the power of sin is the law. But thanks be to God! He gives us the victory through our Lord Jesus Christ.

1 Corinthians 15:56-57

Tips & Extras ∼∼∼∼

• Make the burst behind the cross from gold lamé and/or gold ribbon.

• Use a patterned green fabric for the hillside.

• The letters should be a dark color to stand out from the gold.

• The letters and cross should be the same color to maintain legibility.

Graduation

I (Paul) planted the seed, Apollos watered it, but God made it grow. So neither he who plants nor he who waters is anything, but only God, who makes things grow.

1 Corinthians 3:6-7

Tips & Extras ~~~~

- Hang at a grade school, high school, or college graduation.

- Use white or a neutral off-white for the background.

- The top and bottom color bars and the graduation year can be the school's color. Outline the number with white or black so it stands out from the leaves.

- The leaves can be made from different shades of green—lighter green at the bottom to darker green at the top. The stem/cross could be entirely of dark green, or try the following: Cut the stem/cross from one piece of medium green cotton fabric. Use a brown washable marker to color the cross. As you color towards the bottom, create a blend by coloring lighter and lighter, making fewer and fewer strokes. Then use a small paintbrush loaded only with water to make the ink bleed and create a smooth transition from brown to green (the original fabric color). Practice on scrap first!

- Additional numbers are on page 82.

ISAIAH 40:31

ST. JOHN HIGH

Graduation

Those who hope in the LORD will renew their strength. They will soar on wings like eagles; they will run and not grow weary, they will walk and not be faint.

Isaiah 40:31

Tips & Extras 〰〰

- The abstract eagle's wing can remain abstract by using only three colors to create the banner. Two of the school's colors plus white would be possible choices. (Look at an athletic uniform for a color scheme.) Or the dominant school color, plus tan and white.

- For a more realistic wing, use tan for the wing and a fourth color for the two areas within the square that are not part of the wing. Or lightly shade with a brown marker. If you choose to use two colors in the wing square, balance the banner by using the same colors in the year square—for example, fill the zero with a different color.

- Create a square with the graduation year by using the numbers provided on page 83.

- If the name of the school does not fit on one line, simply make the banner a bit longer and use two lines.

Graduation

Tips & Extras ~~~~~

- This banner should be made to hang horizontally. It would make a good backdrop for the graduation stage and is appropriate for graduation from any level.

- Experiment with color schemes by drawing on paper before making any final fabric choices.

- Don't go "color crazy." A good guideline: Use the same color for the illustration circles and the graduation year. Strongly consider making "Class" this color also. Use another color for both squiggly lines. Use a third color to fill the illustration circles and the zero. This gives the banner balance. Try to use five colors total, including the background.

- Select two illustrations from the four provided: cross, dove, Bible, wheat. Additional numbers are found on page 83.

- Want to use it again next year? Attach the circles and numbers with Velcro and change for a new look. Backing them with fusible interfacing will make them stiff and prevent sagging.

I CHOSE **YOU** TO GO & BEAR FRUIT

FRUIT THAT WILL LAST

**Rev. Michael James
March 18, 2003**

Installation/ Ordination

"You did not choose Me, but I chose you...to go and bear fruit—fruit that will last."

John 15:16

Tips & Extras 〜〜〜

- Use a bright color yellow for the two circles. This acts as a highlight to the words "you" and "last."

- As an option for the tree, look for green fabric that is pre-printed with leaves.

- If this banner is for a specific person's installation or ordination, personalize it with a name and date at the bottom. Use the alphabet on pages 86-87.

Installation/ Ordination

Devote yourself to the public reading of Scripture, to preaching and to teaching. Do not neglect your gift, which was given you.

1 Timothy 4:13-14a

Tips & Extras ∿∿∿

• This is a stained-glass pattern. Plan ahead with color choices to ensure the words will be legible.

• Two possible color schemes:

1) Make the glass all dark shades, primarily purple, blue, green. Highlight sparingly with orange and yellow. The dove and the words will be white. Outline the dove, letters, and each color with black yarn or paint if desired.

2) Make the glass all shades of yellow, orange, and light/pastel colors. The dove is white and the letters are a dark blue or purple. Outline the dove and letters.

• Include the text if desired. Omit the bottom color block if the text is omitted.

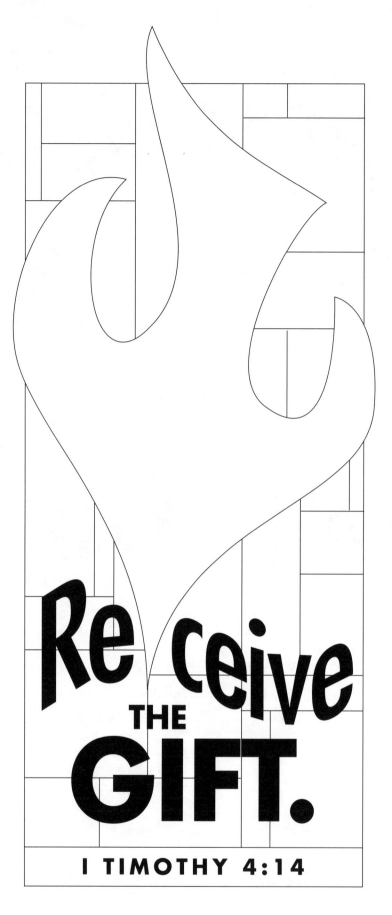

Rev. James Smith
May 24, 2002

Jesus said, "Feed My lambs." Jesus said, "Feed My sheep."
selected from John 21:15-17

Tips & Extras 〰〰〰

• Make sure the letters have enough contrast from the staff and cross so they are easily legible. Outline the letters in the background color for increased contrast.

• Consider gold or silver for the starburst.

• Iron-on fusible makes the script letters easy to cut out and affix to the banner.

• For a beautiful gift, personalize the banner with a name and date.

Lord's Supper

I come, O Savior, to your table,
For weak and weary is my soul;
You, Bread of Life, alone are able
To satisfy and make me whole.
Lord, may your body and your blood
Be for my soul the highest good!

Lutheran Worship #242
Friedrich C. Heyder

Tips & Extras 〜〜〜

- Make the top and bottom trim color metallic gold.

- Instead of cut fabric, make the bread and grapes from yarn. Start on the outer edge of the shape and spiral smaller and smaller until the shape is filled in.

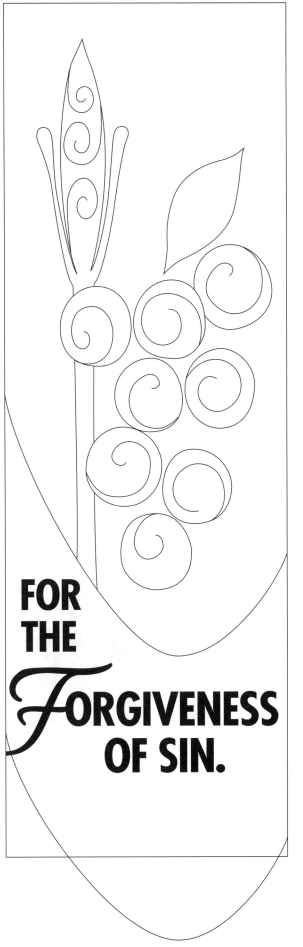

FOR THE *Forgiveness* **OF SIN.**

Lord's Supper

While they were eating, Jesus took bread, gave thanks and broke it, and gave it to His disciples, saying, "Take and eat; this is My body." Then He took the cup, gave thanks and offered it to them, saying, "Drink from it, all of you. This is My blood of the covenant, which is poured out for many for the forgiveness of sins."

Matthew 26:26-28

Tips & Extras ~~~~~

- Make the swirls using a metallic ribbon of the same color as the grape and wheat, respectively.
- Cut the bottom of the banner square or with a curve mimicking the curve of the color field.

Lord's Supper

And He took bread, gave thanks and broke it, and gave it to them, saying, "This is My body given for you; do this in remembrance of Me."

Luke 22:19

Tips & Extras

- This is banner #1 of a pair. The second banner is on the following page.

- The pair could be displayed on opposite sides of the chancel, one above the other in a tall chancel, or one after the other to correspond with Bible study topics.

- Choose colors that are contrasting for the top half and bottom half. Dark blue and white, burgundy and off-white, etc. Make sure the colors of the two banners are the same or work well together.

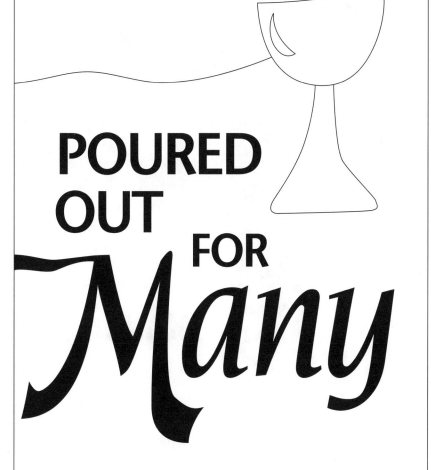

BLOOD OF THE *new* COVENANT, POURED OUT *FOR Many*

Lord's Supper

Then He took the cup, gave thanks and offered it to them, and they all drank from it. "This is My blood of the new covenant, which is poured out for many."

Mark 14:23-24

Tips & Extras ～～～

- This is banner #2 of a pair.
- For other tips, check the notes from banner #1 on the previous page.

Missions

Then Jesus came to them and said, "All authority in heaven and on earth has been given to me. Therefore go and make disciples of all nations, baptizing them in the name of the Father and of the Son and of the Holy Spirit, and teaching them to obey everything I have commanded you. And surely I am with you always, to the very end of the age."

Matthew 28:18-20

Tips & Extras ~~~~~

- The dove should be a color similar to that of the background fabric. Both dark, both light, or one solid color, one patterned.

- Another option is to make the dove gold lamé on a white background. The letters should be a dark color so they are legible from a distance.

- Try outlining the word "Go" with yarn of a slightly darker color than the letters. (If the letters are blue, outline in navy.) Try it before you glue it.

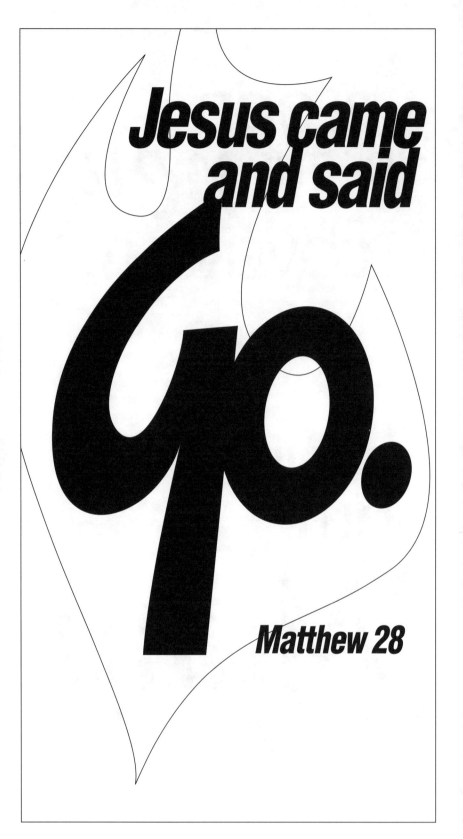

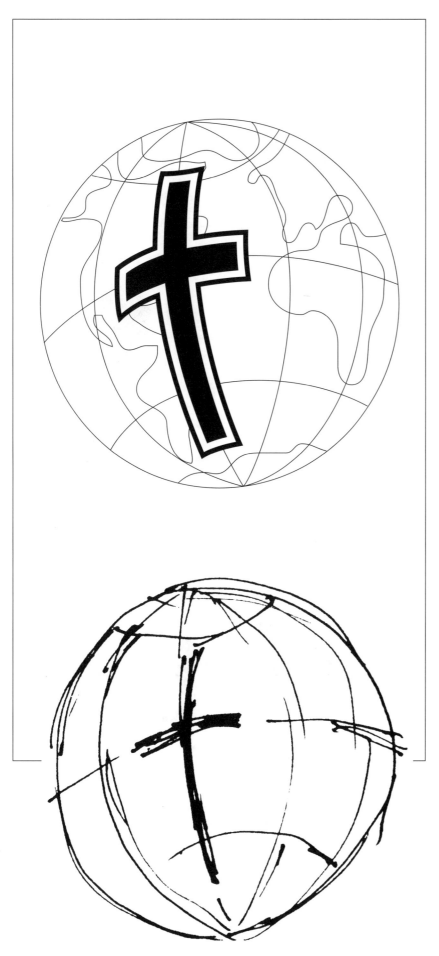

Missions

Declare His glory among the nations, His marvelous deeds among all peoples.

Psalm 96:3

Tips & Extras ~~~~

- There are two ways to illustrate the earth in this banner. The top is a more literal interpretation. Make the water blue, the land green. Glue the land on top of the water. The cross can be anything that stands out from the world—black cross outlined in white, then black; black outlined in white then gold; gold outlined in black then gold; etc. Make the globe lines from white or gold ribbon, yarn, or cord.

- The second is a loose, interpretive earth. Use blue and green yarn combined to make all the lines except the cross. As you work, step back occasionally to see how the banner is progressing. Lines may look better if they are heavier (wider). Make the cross from bright yellow and outline in black.

Praise

Tips & Extras ⌒

- Some possible configurations for these circles:

  1) Arrange all three on one long, narrow banner. This could be hung in an open stairwell, a tall chancel area, off a balcony, in a gathering room, etc.

  2) Have each circle on its own narrow banner. These could be hung along a hallway, down the side of the church itself, or displayed one at a time in successive weeks.

- The line illustrations are optional additions. They work best on individual banners.

- Color idea #1: Make each of the three a different color family on a consistent background. Outer circle is always a dark color, large letter (s,f,s) is a light shade of that color. Inner circle is always gold, small letters are always white, large letter outlined in white.

- Color idea #2: Each background is a different dark color. The outer circle is always white, small letters same as the background. Inner circle is a light shade of the background, large letter is always gold outlined in white.

Praise

Sing praises to God, sing praises;
sing praises to our King, sing praises.

Psalm 47:6

Tips & Extras ~~~~

- Make just one banner and select the illustration most appealing, or make all three and hang as a series.

- Hang banner(s) such as these behind the choir in the church or in the practice room itself.

- Be creative and bold with color selection. Consider this for the guitar: side=bright blue; face=bright pink; hole and strings=yellow; letters=bright purple.

- Or choose classy colors: background=khaki; side=navy; face=cream; hole and strings=navy; letters=white; outline guitar in black.

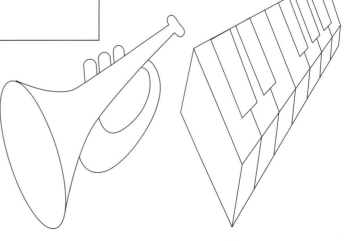

Prayer

He will call upon Me, and I will answer him; I will be with him in trouble, I will deliver him and honor him.

Psalm 91:15

Tips & Extras

- This is a loose visual depiction of Jesus standing with His palms outstretched at His sides.

- A white robe and purple background would look nice. For ease of construction, however, make the entire banner white and glue the purple pieces to the white.

- Use black cord, yarn, or squeeze paint to outline the robe and hands.

- If the pointed corners tend to curl when the banner is hung, hot-glue a 1/2" washer to the back side of each tip.

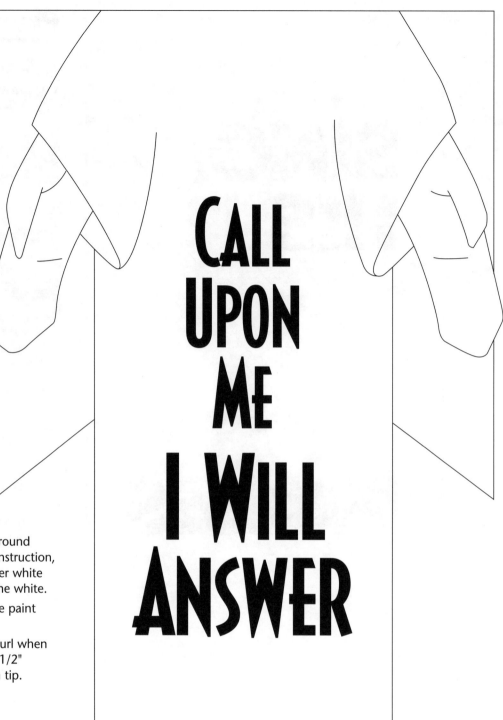

Ask.
Seek.

Knock.

Prayer

"Ask and it will be given to you; seek and you will find; knock and the door will be opened to you. For everyone who asks receives; he who seeks finds; and to him who knocks, the door will be opened."

Luke 11:9-10

Tips & Extras

- This simple banner shows light spilling into a dark room through an opened door.

- A simple color scheme of black, white, and taupe would be fitting for this design, as would three complementary colors.

- The youth room or house would be an appropriate place to display this banner, even after it has been displayed in the church. Seeing a banner in church and in the "living space" would visually bring God's promises into everyday life.

Prayer

"Though the mountains be shaken and the hills be removed, yet My unfailing love for you will not be shaken nor My covenant of peace be removed," says the LORD, who has compassion on you.

Isaiah 54:10

Tips & Extras ~~~~

- This landscape could be designed with a variety of color schemes. From the bottom up, the scene could be 1) sand, dry hills, mountains, bright sky; 2) grass, river, tree-covered hills, snow-covered mountains, blue sky; 3) springtime colors; 4) winter colors; 5) nighttime colors; etc.

- The heart could be distinguished from the landscape in a number of ways: 1) For the heart, use a lighter shade of the same color as the corresponding land area (like the grayscale illustration above). 2) Use solid colors for the landscape and matching colors with a pattern for the areas that make the heart. 3) Construct the banner without the heart. Then make a cardboard or paper template that covers the entire banner and cut out where the heart should be. Lay the banner flat. Lightly mist the heart area with white spray paint, holding the can about two feet above the banner. Point the can out, not down. Just barely press the spray tip so the paint spits more than sprays. Practice on scraps first!

FATHER, KEEP US.

Prayer

The LORD is good, a refuge in times of trouble. He cares for those who trust in Him.

Nahum 1:7

Tips & Extras ~~~~

These banners can be hung one at a time or hung as a series along the side of the sanctuary, along a hallway, in a fellowship hall, one above the other in an alter area with a high ceiling, etc.

- The internal circular pattern of this banner presents a fresh representation of the eternal nature of God that often is represented by the whole circle. You also could delete the circular pattern and connect the ends of the cord to form a "whole" shape.

- As a series, the three could be done in the same colors or complementary colors. Two good choices would be navy blue, dark green, and burgundy or slate blue, taupe, and dark tan.

- A simple way to form the illustrations would be to use cord. Use a lighter shade of the dark background color, white, or black. Several strands of yarn works well also.

- The letters should contrast strongly with the background—more than or equal to the contrast between the image and background.

Prayer

She will give birth to a son, and you are to give Him the name Jesus, because He will save His people from their sins.

Matthew 1:21

Tips & Extras

- This banner is the second in a series of three that represent the Holy Trinity.
- The internal circular pattern of this banner presents a fresh representation of the eternal nature of God that often is represented by the whole circle. You also could delete the circular pattern and connect the ends of the cord to form a "whole" shape.
- Please refer to the comments that accompany the "Father, Keep Us" banner on page 67.

SPIRIT, GUIDE US.

Prayer

"But the Counselor, the Holy Spirit, whom the Father will send in My name, will teach you all things and will remind you of everything I have said to you."

John 14:26

Tips & Extras ~~~~~

- This banner is the third in a series of three that represent the Holy Trinity.

- The internal circular pattern of this banner presents a fresh representation of the eternal nature of God that often is represented by the whole circle. You also could delete the circular pattern and connect the ends of the cord to form a "whole" shape.

- Please refer to the comments that accompany the "Father, Keep Us" banner on page 67.

Processional

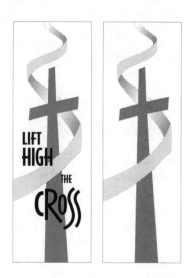

Tips & Extras 〰️

- Processional banners look wonderful as two-sided banners. To do this, cut two backgrounds from the same heavy material. Lay the two pieces together, right sides facing. Sew together on three sides, leaving the top unfinished. Turn the material right-side-out and sew the hanging casement. Cut out two of each banner piece and attach to both sides.

- To create the "shadowed" ribbon: Use a cotton fabric, watercolor paint, and a 1" (or larger) brush. If the fabric is white or tan, try using a little bit of any color paint. With colored fabric, use the same color paint with black added.

  Cut the pattern from paper. Tape waxed paper to your work surface. Tape a section of fabric (larger than the pattern) to your waxed paper. Wet the entire piece with the brush using only water (no paint). Starting at one end of the fabric, blend the paint from dark to light towards the center. Let the fabric dry completely before moving or cutting. Practice on scraps first!

- To make the letters stand out from the cross, outline them with a ribbon or yarn that matches the background fabric.

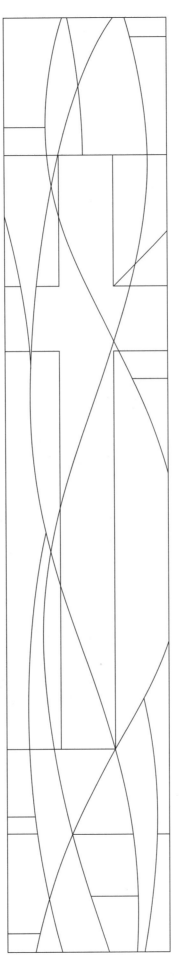

Processional

"I am the light of the world. Whoever follows Me will never walk in darkness, but will have the light of life."

John 8:12

Tips & Extras ~~~~~

- This banner can be used for processionals, displayed permanently, or made on a small scale for use as altar paraments or even on a stole.

- Colors should be chosen to replicate the look of stained-glass.

- Use yellow and bright oranges for the cross; blues, greens, and purples for the background. Make a few of the smaller background squares a bright color for some variation.

- Use colors of the same family (i.e., different types of blues) for each sweeping band (see the grayscale image above at right).

- Before cutting fabric, use markers to try different color schemes on photocopies of the design.

Stewardship

Commit your way to the LORD; trust in Him and He will do this: He will make your righteousness shine like the dawn, the justice of your cause like the noonday sun.

Psalm 37:5-6

Tips & Extras

- How does that arrow work? 1) The hanging casement will be made only with the fabric that does not make the arrow. Sew the hanging casement. 2) Insert the wooden dowel rod. 3) Use paint stir-sticks to make the arrow brace. It should follow the top two edges and each side edge. The sticks should extend below the dowel rod by 1". Following the diagram, screw sticks to the dowel rod at each +, glue stick to stick at each •, and fabric to stick along the squiggle lines. Once the arrow is glued to the sticks, the dowel rod is no longer removable.

- The burst is a secondary design element and its color should be similar to the background so it doesn't detract from the focus of the banner.

- The sweeping shape within the arrow should be subtle also. It could be shiny white on flat white, light yellow on white, texture on no texture.

Stewardship

"This is to My Father's glory, that you bear much fruit, showing yourselves to be My disciples."

John 15:8

Tips & Extras ~~~~

- This banner, along with the following two, could be used as a group for a weekend retreat, conference, or gathering.
- Use individually during a stewardship month or program.
- The grapes can all be made from the same fabric. Outline each grape with yarn or squeeze paint to separate them from each other.
- Or make each grape from a different shade or pattern of purple.
- Make the leaf using a horizontally patterned fabric. Change the direction of the pattern to distinguish the two sides of the leaf.

Stewardship

Praise the LORD, O my soul; all my inmost being, praise His holy name.

Psalm 103:1

Tips & Extras ~~~~~~

- Use as part of the series or individually during a choir concert, etc.
- Make the staff lines from a color similar to the background so they are secondary in visual impact. Gold would be appropriate.
- The notes could be the same or similar colors, or similar to the grapes as explained on the previous page.

Stewardship

"Let your light shine before men, that they may see your good deeds and praise your Father in heaven."

Matthew 5:16

Tips & Extras 〰️

- Use as part of the series or individually for evangelism Sunday, etc.
- If used as a series, consider making the flames, staff lines, and grape leaf all gold lamé while using the same color(s) for the candles, notes, and grapes.

Wedding

Be completely humble and gentle; be patient, bearing with one another in love. Make every effort to keep the unity of the Spirit through the bond of peace. There is one body and one Spirit—just as you were called to one hope when you were called—one Lord, one faith, one baptism.

Ephesians 4:2-5

Tips & Extras 〰️

- Look for a background fabric that has a subtle inlaid pattern, especially if the banner is a gift that will later be displayed in the home. The appearance will be elegant.

- "one" needs to be a light color that does not compete at all with the script letters that overlay it. Gold lamé is a good choice for "one" and the cross.

- Let's be frank: The script letters are no picnic to cut out. Iron-on fusible and felt fabric are the easiest to work with. The beautiful result makes it worthwhile!

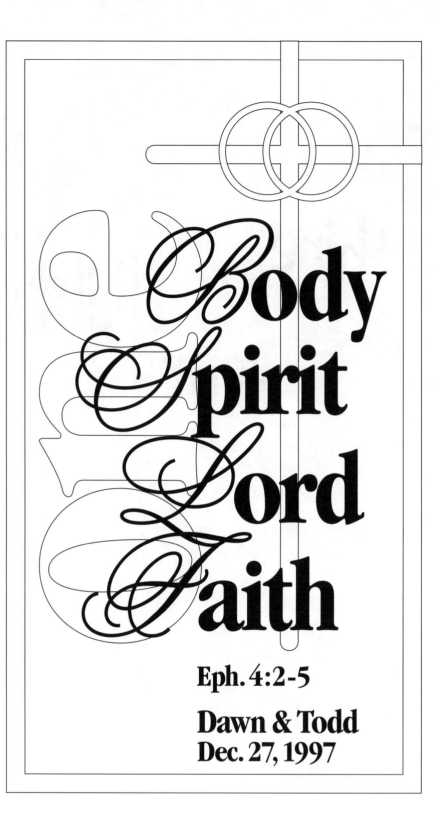

Body
Spirit
Lord
Faith

Eph. 4:2-5

Dawn & Todd
Dec. 27, 1997

Colossians 3:12-17

**Theodore & Connie
May 25, 2002**

Wedding

Forgive as the Lord forgave you. And over all these virtues put on love, which binds them all together in perfect unity. ... And whatever you do ... do it all in the name of the Lord Jesus, giving thanks to God the Father through Him.

Colossians 3:13-14, 17

Tips & Extras 〰

- This is an atypical wedding text, but a beautiful one nonetheless. Take time to read the reference in its entirety.
- The border can be the same color as the letters.
- Wide gold ribbon makes a quick and easy cross.
- Gold cord can trim the border and outline the rings.
- Use a variety of gold trim styles, but make sure the "golds" match.

Wedding

For this reason a man will leave his father and mother and be united to his wife, and they will become one flesh.

Genesis 2:24

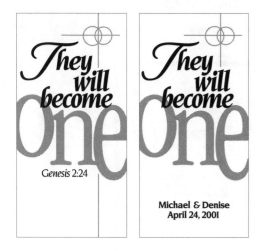

Tips & Extras

- This banner could be made for use in the church during any wedding by including only the scripture reference or made for a specific couple by including their names and wedding date.

- "They will become" and any other words should be the darker of the two colors chosen for the banner.

- Gold metallic fabric is a good choice for the word "one." Use iron-on fusible for metallic fabrics to prevent fraying.

- Ribbon makes a quick and easy cross. Try gold, especially if "one" is gold.

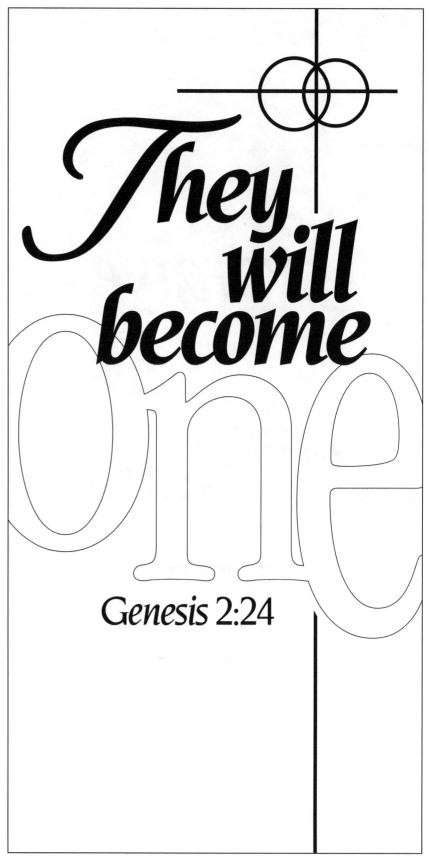

A Cord of
3 strands
is NOT
quickly
broken.

Ecc. 4:7-12

Michael & Denise
April 24, 2001

Wedding

Though one may be overpowered, two can defend themselves. A cord of three strands is not quickly broken.

Ecclesiastes 4:12

Tips & Extras

- Use two colors: one for the "3" and scripture text, a second for the other words.

- When making the background, allow for a hanging casement on the bottom edge. Sew the bottom the same as the top. Use a 1" dowel for the top and bottom rods, making sure to have extra rod to the left of the banner.

- This left edge is where the braided cord is attached. Start by screwing three lengths of heavy cord to the back of the top dowel, three inches from the left side.

- Working on the floor, lay the dowel behind 2 chair legs with the braid in between them. This will allow you to pull tightly as you work. Braid slightly longer than the actual banner length and tie the braid with a rubberband.

- Move back up to the table. With your banner face down, insert both dowel rods. Allow the braid to hang past the bottom rod. Screw it to the rod so when hung, it will not sag. Trim off the excess braid.

- Put glue on all cord ends so they will not unravel.

- Omit the cord if it doesn't suit you!

Wedding

May the God who gives endurance and encouragement give you a spirit of unity among yourselves as you follow Christ Jesus, so that with one heart and mouth you may glorify the God and Father of our Lord Jesus Christ.

Romans 15:5-6

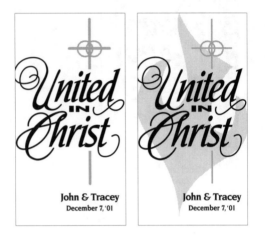

Tips & Extras

- If the background dove will be included, this is a beautiful method: Make the background a smooth, flat white fabric. The dove fabric would be a shiny white jacquard with a subtle pattern. Iron on the dove using fusible web.

- Center the couples' names and date under the cross.

- Make the cross from gold ribbon.

- If you want the dove to stand out a bit more, outline it with white squeeze paint.

- Felt is the easiest to work with when cutting detailed letters such as these.

- A razor blade knife is an excellent tool that can cut in tight, enclosed spaces. Be sure to use cardboard underneath when cutting.

Unless the LORD builds the house, its builders labor in vain.

Psalm 127:1

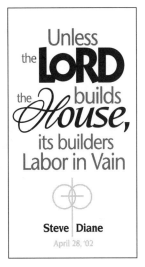

Tips & Extras

- Make all the letters the same color, or ...
- Make "Lord" and "House" one color and the rest of the words a second color. These two colors should be similar in value (one not too much lighter than the other).
- Make the cross and rings from gold ribbon or cord. Be patient when gluing cord—be sure not to stretch it. It has to lay in the glue and dry flat.

Anniversary, p. 20

1 2 3 4 5 6 7 8 9 0

Anniversary, p. 20

1 2 3 4 5 6 7 8 9 0

Graduation, p. 50; Anniversary, p. 21

1 2 3 4 5 6 7 8 9 0

1234567890

Anniversary, p. 22

1234567890

Graduation, p. 51

1234567890

Graduation, p. 52

abcdefg
hijklmn
opqrstu
vwxyz
ʻ,:;12 34
567890

Futura Bold

A B C D E F
G H I J K L
M N O P
Q R S T U
V W X Y Z

Futura Bold

abcdef
ghijklm
nopqrst
uvwxyz
,':.;1234
567890

Novarese Bold

ABCDE
FGHIJK
LMNOP
QRSTU
VWXYZ

Novarese Bold

Notes

Notes

Notes

Notes

Notes

Notes